FYI

Rhetorical Word Sculpture

FYI

Rhetorical Word Sculpture

Grant H. Blackwell

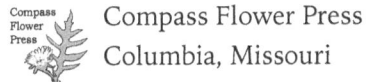

Compass Flower Press
Columbia, Missouri

Published by
Compass Flower Press
Columbia, Missouri

Cover photography by Peter Yankowski
Title lettering by Exia Lin Bailey and Grant H. Blackwell
Graphite portrait of author by Exia Lin Bailey

Library of Congress Control Number: 2025902613
ISBN: 978-1-951960-67-4

The test of any organizing principle is its success in rendering specifics not its status as abstract generality.

—Stephen Jay Gould, *Time's Arrow, Time's Cycle. Myth and Metaphor in the Discovery of Geological Time*, (Jerusalem-Harvard Lectures, London) Harvard University Press, 1987

Propaedeutic

propaedeutic - A. adj. Pertaining to or of the nature of preliminary instruction; supplying the knowledge or discipline introductory or preliminary to some art or science; preliminarily educational.

The most interesting situations can usually be expressed as a What-if question…

—Stephen King

What if each piece in a poetry collection was titled a three letter initialism? And what if each three letter work was composed only of words starting with the letters of that particular initialism in a repeating pattern from beginning to end? What if this compound alliteration was used to describe the title or an aspect of the initialism's essence? And what if every letter was used in the collection without repeating a word?

For Your Information: Rhetorical Word Sculpture began with these what ifs evolving to a self questioning challenge of, What if this isn't possible? And as most of my art begins with the varying question of possibility, it was reaction to these restrictions that gave FYI voice.

Completing the entire manuscript without repeating words meant FYI would be unabridged and even slang. Introduction of foreign language, including dead language, was done to increase my word base and utilize concepts without English translation. Usage of historical events and terms, another reaction to the restriction I imposed on FYI, further enriched the word base with ideas, objects, and people no longer referred to, or not in the same way.

As need arose, self imposed art rules were chipped away and my parameter of using a word once loosened to allow them in a different poem and in an alternate part of speech. Initialisms containing the letters X and J are not included as these letters are sparsely applied as the cornerstone of words in our tongue.

FYI also required a creative license with syntax, part of speech, case, and number. Proper nouns that could be "bent" into synonyms were stretched to become common ideas and "new" forms of words were created and applied as long as the intended meaning was conveyed.

FYI is impressionistic in its diction so epigraphs were given to additively sculpt context and tone. The three letters represent a tricycle's balance, the golden ratio, and rule of thirds. Sonically the compound alliteration achieved through repetition of letter and juxtaposition of languages created a sound quality suited for performance. However other literary devices lend for a disparate experience on the page. The phrasing of this poetry is rap, with graffiti invoked by the three letter crew names pervasive in hip hop. The specific initialisms chosen were included first, as on an array of subject matter for well roundedness of the whole; and second, as concepts familiar enough to the reader that a cursory knowledge could be assumed, as there has to be a definition in order to redefine. "GHB" and "BBL" are included as debut concepts, the former being my initials and the latter Big Black Lies, the visual art collective (bbl is technically a measure of volume denoting half a barrel).

Politically correct "PC" or Presto Change-o was added later and is the only two-letter initialism. There are exactly three pieces that use one letter and the twenty two total pieces represent branches on the tree of life. *FYI: Rhetorical Word Sculpture* is dedicated to my parents and to ExL's three Rs.

RWS

Rhetorical Word Sculpture ("Ideophonically") *Litho-Literary slang;* **noun**; Forms: Rhetorical Word Sculpture Work.

Researched Well, ston retrospective we'd seen
Rishi waylaid so raspy welded stelae rasped
with the stomatic,
Rodin wynn spoken raillery of Webster santo's niche;
prolepsis in grandiloquent gist gisant originally
original process of semantic scultile technique,
tableaux
or those inference installments forged of phonetic
facet figuration
as free standing stabiles formalized for effect;

Chorten correctly, combined formature of Mead-
mache monument and MastoDonatello
in master suite; macaronic in modern usage
ebonic ebauchoir, i.e, explicitly toreutic telestich
esp. in relief of response elicited,
or in round about alabaster alouds engraved on
or as hard material molding;

Calder condition or quality intaglio of consonant
characters and vowel poesy
cast in plastering of Paris
as to persuade design produced
operative in planar duality's patterned discourse,
diorism,
and dilogy's 3D et cetera circumjacent the syllabic
foreshortening;

Any artificial language art extravagance
erected Anti-Semantic,

or referenced wax silhouette ritornello and verbum sat
bronzed between act and thinker in abstract,
or representative Wallace Stevens riddle,
witticism
or satire related Wellerism see: prayer
battle rap
and the alliterative compound acronym.

—Grant H. Blackwell

Table of Contents

POW

I turned my hand around inside the straps, and finally got the tip of my fingers up nearby my moustache and yanked and pulled my head back yanking the gag off my mouth. I hollered out…

—Bobby Seale

A patriotic orphan warning the political ostriches
worshiping protest opprobrium wrapped plutocrats
ordering wall paneled orles widening Pavlov's-obedient-
Weltanschauung-plot.

The Orwellian writ's pygmalion oligarchs
wallet pluralising an Ophthalmic-wool-pulley's
Oppenheimer windfall-profiting.

An opposite Warsaw Pact's oppressively wardened-
protocol ownership, waving plutonium's
oscillating waste pail osmosis and wizzening

the Pacific orca whale predicament's
oily Wiltshire petro-oops!-Watergate pulse
oddly whizzing past the ozone's whole peccadillo.

An orientation weaponizing paranoia's ordeal wound
and perpetrators occlude window paned Orion warmth
proving only will power opposes wily patrician offensives
when public opinion wanes.

StL

As I drive around Saint Louis and see all the vacant lots and blocks and rundown and boarded up buildings, I ask myself, what caused all this?

—Ron Fagerstrom

La Selva trapped leather sale and a trade luff
shaped this landscape's stratified transmontane lich-stone tilth and latifundia.
Securing the tract license swimmingly
Thneedville's lumber safari's threshed Lorax sycamore tons–
log skinning their luxuriously-synthetic-tundra-longitude's–
stagecoach-travel-leeway-silt.
The telos liquidation sooner than laggingly.

Servile Toussant L' Ouvertures stomped trustee Leclerc's striding Tudors,
letting secessionists then loricate the sheared territory's
Louisiana sugar trove, Lord Sheffield trumping Limoges's
saintly titled Lewis site and transported letters, suds, timber, lard
and salt telepharages. Livestock sustaining the Talmadge law's
shamefully traduced lashes and syncretized tourniquet linens,
a short time later,

state's truce lapsed. Sherman triumphing
Lee surrendering tattered lunettes and signed treaties lured
the southern trolley leveraging slaves, turning loose station throng
limbs and slowly traversing the Laclede steamer turbine's lodestar.
A sundown town,
legitimizing the searching thralls lividly seeking transformative labor.

Shortages teemed limpidly. So the laniferous shouldered a tough load
settling Theodore Link's striker tableau
and lubricating Sir Toppem lacuna's, spacially too little swath
tucked littorally.

Stuck there, lalophobia subsidized trepidations,
and the lurid spritz-tan lepers shot to Ladue's senile tradition,
lair separating a total lop sided tabescence,
lugging the seven thirty lineage's, scaffolding thruster–
Lindbergh spirit
thwarting Langston's scheduled Tuskegee launch.

Sadly, throughout the lumpen, Soul-Train lining slum tenements,
lavish sneakers treasured like sterling trinkets
luxate the STEM trade lacking-schools tracking a learner.

The supernal tranter's lummy-sneak thief latch string.
A toothsome lick sacrilege and telesis, leastwise–

Satyrias and tawdry ladies shaking that lipid
soiling the Tina Loop Star's tamed livery stable toponym.
Loan sharking tender's legal
and Templars leech spruce Tula layoffs
sans a true lachrymal semblance, tempering luck a stiff
Tulia litigation and shrievalty.

The teflon Lumina sirens trail a lanated,
Swisher tearing lime spliff taxonomy's lay sprout–
tossin the lasso squadron ticket lottery's
spurious tabloid libel.

Set tripping loudly

Stan Tookie's L.A. sapphire troop lodges sip Tussin
and leak Seville trunk laser scrum-*talionis*
lexing,
a scarlet-tied-shell-toe lokin' surreptitious
and targeting lieutenants stifling

the teen lamb,
sada te lifer,
sardine tin lemmings
Schlafly tub lathering and shuttle trekking lightly.

Shorties take losses siring toddlers lackadaisically
splurging textile limburger spread thin. Literally,
Senegal trick labyrinth's spearmint tasting Lorillard smoke
triggering lung sarcoma treatment largesse,
sourer than lemon-shogun takeout's
London-Son triglyceride lunches.

The suey-tarian Last Supper's
top lentil stomach teaser leasing
a suicidal thought lilt's
steel tope landing spectacle.

Tourism lauding the Slay throne locale's
second tier levees
splashing a threatened lattice's shoddy thoroughfare lanes
shredding tires,
leaning sedan tubes lumpy,
and slanting transmigration lukewarm.

The smart talk leaving stoop terraces
and lickettey-splitting tragic Lambert's Shawshank tunnel.

Lately, snotty tissue Lesslie Spadden tribulations–
linger the stinky turd loo subdivision's tribalist liniment,

Strom Thurman lilliputians side-tongue lipping
a solipsistic typhoon's–
lyrical slur taunting lunacy.

Schadenfreude and Teutons
looting the sequestered turf's

Lemony Snicket tranquility locus
locking Selassies,
and truncating the Lego skyscraper-
tattered limbo surrounding
the thrifty lunatic Sanford tizzies laterally
shuffling Texaco lots.

cDr

What I dig's invisible. I'm its teacher. It's my student.
I'll tell you, ain't nothin quite as beautiful as music.

—Eyedea

Cri du renard's copyright ditched,
release cloned desktop recording.

A cassette disposal renaissance
and current declarative reported
carpe diem recital confection.

Decibel refraction of a Casio din's
rounded circumference and diameter
ratio cadenced–

digi reading of a carbon devoid reel
condensed diaphragm rhapsody.

The chanted dark room crystallized
diacritic rap classic diction.

RCA chord and dolby relieving a Cali
dream record company directed
robbery.

ThC

So stupid minded.

—Marvin Gaye

Teal Honda Civic tinted hundred
cruising turnpikes hurriedly carrying two hebetic Cardinal Tweety's
histrionic construct

temporal hardiment's collocated tryst,
headlong cohortatives, these here comically testified Hollister
California's Theo Huxtable centile.

Tidily hegemonic,
clothing typically hip-hop casual. Turkish herrings clanking
the Tory Holt caftan twins' haughtily creased toggery.

Hereditarily consanguine,
tagged Henry and Charles Turner. Hedonistically curious,
and truant habitually cutting Truman High classes-

together haggling,
the cousins truly hated campus third hour conformity's
teetotalling history crap.

Thursday, the hooky *cortege* trundled the hidrotic Celcii's
tectonically humid consequence. Tragi hearing a Crenshaw-
tune harmony's cranked tambor.

Hash continence tenoring the humbug's commissive thema.
Hybrid compelling them herbally.
"Call Tim," Hank clumsily tantrummed-handling clutch tensely-honking
cursing traffic,
and honoring the countermanded towrow's holophrastic colloquy-

the theriacally helpful Charley's T9 hacked a cell tower's
hesperian columna, tocsins harping the connect Timothy,
Hank's commodiously talented hay clocker trolling a hoop court's
tort hindered comex.

"Tight!" hooted the confirmation's Titan hat. Charles telling the helmsman, "Cool," the tandem hugged the circuitous thruway hazards careening til Heman cobblestones tophaceously harkened a consummated trip.

Hoppin Converse Taylor HIs, Charles traipsed the hardened concrete, tween-a-hunter-Caddy-Tonka's hubcap coruscations-thundering Hova Carter trilogy's "Hoes, Cash, Thaler."

Hustling ceruleans,

a tonus Hoover clique tally hung cornice tented hunching.

Craps transpired,
hostile and chillin Tar Heel cotton tees and hoof caps
tippin Hennessey cups,
torchin the Hindu Cush taboo's
humorous Chris Tucker holy wood.

Tiny hailed Craig, thetically hands clasped
and the timid held contraband. Tommy Hil
cargo trousers hiking contentedly tracing his compact, tepidly-
"Holla Cuzzo," tapered.

Hereupon comfortable and taciturn, hombres convened-
tendron harvest copped, they huddled chassis thoughts
hankering cigars and
therefore, Hankooks corralled-
touring a Halliburton-coal-tanker's heightened clearance
toward the hyaline counter top
hoarding Cosmo-Tribunes and Hostess cake taxed heartily.

Custies trickled harassing a cinnamon-Tamarin Hall clerk,
twitchin' hazel contacts, a trainee hella comely
tangerine halter and counting the till.

Hushedly cupid took hold, Charles trumpetting
the "Hey Cutie," Thurston Harris catcall.

Tickled, honey countered thrasonically humbling Chuck's terse hubris,
and the crowd's throaty-hyena cheshires tittered.

Having the cigarillo,
tushies hit cushion tuffets, happy camping the thrumming hoopty's cabin-
thumping hypogeal-chronic treble's hypnosis, conjuring tarantism,
and the hempen comrades twisted a hurtum-cultus tea humidor,
chiefin' a timer
and hazily coasting the transiently hollow callousness.

Tangentially however,
a city-trooping house Carl's tac-nodal Hemi came thither,
hence corporals toting hodometer collimation's
Tutsi homing calibrator,
and tabulating the hamstrung compatriots, trucking hastily,
the Chrysler tailed hitch
calmly tooting the halogen candle tête-à-tête hinted cuffs.

"Terrific!" hissed the console technician's hooligan culpability
timorous,
hilariously chewing Trident hesitating compliance
and thurifying the handy cologne's torrential halitus confabulating.

Terrified, Henry cowered tacitly
heeding the cable's Trayvon homily circulation,
and trembling a horrent condolence, touched his
corrugation textured, hilt concealed-thumper's handle.

Cheeks tearing heavy,
Chuck theandrically hides the culverine throbbing heinously
and cogitates a trial's heroically continuous Tasmanian holocaust
they considered Toby's halt Cobain, so their Hopson's Choice
was Talladega Hanley's Corridor.

Trenchantly, Hitler's car tore hunnishly, crowding,

truculent horn cymbals-
a tarsal hammered carburetor's traction-
and hirring continental theatrics of
hormonal clenched torsos,
the hereford crusaded thrilled,
hounding the consortium's taxi-
haulin-

a Cutlass threaded Henry's cross traversary's-
hyper-condensated tarmac hydroplaning

a collision t-boning the homiez carriage
"thwack!" and horrisonant crunches
throwing him catapulted and tumbling,
hurling the cockpit's trampled humanity.

Charles transcended the harrowing crash
thrombotically horizontal
caution tape, howling Caprices and towers
hurdled to cordon the tousled,
heli-choppered thoracic hemorager's
compunction-transfusing Humana copays.

Theurgically healed to completion,
though haunted, and comporting-triage-hospital-cots
thus handi capped,

traumatized, hallucinating and conscious
the tugging hindsight cartwheeled trinitarian
as Henry consolidated Thanatos,
the humation cemetery,
and a tulip heaped coffin
transuding heuristic contrition.

DVd

Livingstone, the famous African Missionary and a medical doctor, says syphilis dies out in the African interior. It seems incapable of permanence in any form, in persons of pure African blood.

—J.A. Rogers

A debility vowing delinquent's defective venefice
and delegation.

Don't visit the dimwit decubitus voir dire's
depauperizing vanguard of duplicities
denoting a viper's death draped vallus
and dooming the diaphorically Victorian.

A dose dichotomy's vicissitude debarked damocles.

Valor dilating dacoity and vaulting a deceitful demophile
vouchsafed.

Druid doctors Vinn diagramming a debut's
venomously dry diaphysis valley
dangling the depraved Vlad Dracula's
Daumeresque viscera dinner date.

A vaccine detracting Derrick vortex. Definitely

don't visit the depredative Doolittle villains
doling a doodad vivisection's diversion diagnostically,

the vaticide department
DARPA vibrating a diabolic draught volley's defalcation,
dictating the vulgus desisting dendrite voodoo,

and Doogie's diathesis vaginally dissect domestic,
vaguely drugged,

direct variable damseldom,
discreetly vulturish,

ditto the dope vanquished detainee's darky village
and dubiously duplicate Venezuelan disorders.

Don't visit the dandruff detergent's vesicating dermatology
desquamating visages,
and denying documents.

Violently DNA dabblers veil a discerptibly deformed-
Vaisya despondence
and Darwin's vampirically devout
disguise the vitriol dabbed dairy visna derivative's
dreadful vet dossier.

Dividend vexed deductible viands demurring
their due and victimized Dufresnes.

Didascalically,
a vermin diced diversity's via dolorosa
don't visit a dungeon.

Dusky voles didder Delano's vitelline dally-
discharging VD dedimus verdicts deftly
deanships vamp the doubter demographics-
vanishing Dogon Dodos
and vector diasporas delve the voluminous destination's
despondence vicinity decried a dizzy voter-
doing diddly versus dacnomaniacal dispity
vacating the dearly departed vault ditches,
digging vanfuls,
and divvying decomposed ventral diamonds
defrosting a vegetable Disney's debridement vial decanter.

Don't visit the dispendious deli, vamoose
and discern a deviant vandal developed decoy version

duping dire vagrant dorms,
and draining vinaceous desudations.

A doozie validated Dow dealer
virtually dental drilling viewing ducts for droppers.

Vicariously dirty Denmark vapor drizzles depo vat depletion
of Darth Vader's-diaper-dandy-venerated daughter descendants
drowning in Depakote-vended docility's
deficiency vehicle.

Don't visit the drearily draconian valise
and defend disclosure veridically.

A disgusted dad's vociferous dysphagia,
debunking the vulnerary dissertation duppies
vacillating dude dolichocephalics volatile derelict dromedaries
vividly dimming deities vulnerably dumb
deaf visionless donors.

MMA

It is as though, the "below the belt restriction states, the testicles have nothing whatsoever to do with this contest." In reality however, this contest is only about the genetic power of the testicles.

—Dr. Frances Cress Welsing

Monster Mashings and mutilation.

Malice afore's myrmecic mandible assaulting
Marvelous-

Marv Albert's Mcgwire marked Andro mafia
montaging anger/

and mangling a mesh Ace mummified Mungo's anima mundi
moskeneering the avoirdupois memento mori
and adorning mata mata adjudication's minstrel medium.

The apropos of Mike Mike's abetted McCarthyist moxy
abbreviating the mercurial,
and mirroring the aggressive millennium's mujahid
attrition match mano-a-mano's main attractive microcosm.

Molesting all marbles morally/
appetizing minced meat atrophies.

Mickey and Mallory's agape moratorium-mapping Asia'a
maddening March arena's
mordant Marine athletics the miscreant munchkins adored/

a Mighty Mouse ambushing, Marty Mcfly antagonist mallet.

Martel's aggravated and mollywhopped mundanity aggrandized-
mud menage of the arrogant mean mugging adrenal metabolite-
McMahon announced mimicking
Mohammad Ali's mat mopping affrays.

A Mandalay mirage alluring
mayweathered mystique's alpha male mannequin
archetypes–
munching methyl-aldehyde martinis.
The morphine addictions moribund metier.

Apartheid Macho's mammothly adversarial Moscow Macarena
attacking moniker and mortal anathemas
merciless–

miscegeny's Arlington mascot monetized
Andean molehills,
mountaineering an Atlas mire magnetized absolutism
myopia and meritocracy.

An aspirated mob-moshing the armchaired-maxim's
Magnavoxed autopsy. Mid mast,

Adidas medal's mulctifying avulsion medley
and maximizing the acrimony's metonymically mooched–
admission muscle–
                                        mass–
America's mesmerized audience the mortared Mohicans.

An ambidextrous messiah's
mumbled aphasic moan muffling "avuncles"
and a mild mandingo ambiance.

Modernity's monstrous attitude.

CNN

If push came to shove, I could lose all self respect and become a reporter.

—Charles Barkley

Conceived notion notariqon concerning nil-noologizing
the carnal nidor's nundating crude neroli neplus contrived,
naphthene nozzled compendium non nobis.

Chousery's neck noosing, chokey nutshell Niagara
cascading the nympholeptic nincompoop's
constantly nebulous nightly

covering nothing notable 'cept a necrotically nuanced
catastrophe's nasty noir channel nychthemeron narrative
coronach-
narrowing a Napoleon cyborg nihilist nook

censoring naughty Nagas conveniently
neutering Newtons cache a nugacious novelty.

Comstock negating nubilation's coaxingly neon Nicene
Creed noyade-
nominating the commodore naval naumachia's Churchillian
neter
nudging a cosmetically nobel, nomad circus nimbly navigating
continents naturalizing native cerebral neurons nationalistic.

Cameras?

Nazi novem cartridge's nearsighted Nikon convergence.
Naah, normalities cloud nine nixing nomocracy.

A nephanalyzed cumulo-nimbus nark consulate's
nominative Nabisco cracker nacho nutritionally,

Candy's niche never cast new negro Chris & Neefs

nonplussedly camouflaging nervous Nellie country's
nulliparous nescience,
and clamoring nauseatingly narcissistic cacophony's,
noisomely noxious Carlyle nails nicking
the chalkboard nickelode.

Nonetheless,
"Cauterize NATO's nemeses!" cry nobly needling/
Cronkite nitwits,
needlessly cueing noon noddy's
complicitly neurotic Nimrods,
cluelessly neaping natty captioned nether notices
crawling natantly nominal Colorado nugget nominals,
the climbing nortenos,
and nonsensical Chicano nisi.

The NSA's circumspect next NASA cynosure nauts,
nakedly canarding Nerf noggins cringing-
the Nasdaq nadir's cajolery nitpicked nouveau.

A clinical, nearly narcotine customized napalm nosiness.

Contempt's notanda novel clustering nowadays,
negligent criminal's nifty number choreo-
nutating notoriously caustic Nagasaki nivosity-
and cartographing nuclear nanism's corpuscular neophytes.

A charnel Nuremberg, netflick chronicled nictation-
nympho chattering of noetic novacaine coalitions
negotiating the napping chattel's nostril nostrums,
cursorily nuddling neat cattle nares Norman circa
the nineteen Neanderthal century's, nirvanically
Nicaraguan crack noel

and natiform Colonel North's numbing contra node.
Nocturning Chernobyl naivete notwithstanding,

a contorted nepotist Nordic's caucasoid niece nabbing,

case naggery necessitating
correspondents neologing niceties concurrently nettling
no one-

Celia's nubility nests a courtesan net's nutmegging collet,
and nonesuch nudity conundrums note-nonchalant costra nostras
nursing controversy's
Natalie nomen-clatured Nzinga nefandus
circumscribing nauches nocuous cozeners, Nay,

Nephew clansmen not naming coarse Nandi's neither.

Mrs.

Married women are kept women and they are beginning to find it out.

—Lord Pearsall Smith

May rose smitten monandry's ramified Saturday
minister rental
sermonizing Mister Roosevelt's shimmering,
mood ring stigmatized marzipan recipe
and the snarled mooring rope's smooched Macy's
registrar.

Sex moon restraining stale-mate recital
sworn-monogamy and rayon suit's meretricious raiment
soiree's maundy
ravelling the scalene Mendelsohn recessional's
sauntering Maestoso regaled *sobriquet.*

Ma rupa sakti's murdered Robertas
softly in minute rice showered mactations rattling
strung muffler's ruffled saffron mantillaed radix squaw
maudlin.

Rhododendron and seneschals mulling the rear seat-
miscible Rosa status meld ritual.

Sequacious modernity's requisite syndrome
maiden rending surname misnomers rather selfishly,
marking relationships successfully marshaling religion
standardized, mansard roof sandwiching,
marriage rank sadism.

Myopic retainment sorority's muster roll supplement
murdering Roberta soft in minute rice showers
manifesting rote spouse-hood
mens rea saddled

muliebrous rinse a saucepan
meal roast subordinate role spoofing Mercari rock slippers

ma rupa sakti mending a rutted sash mortgaged,
ripped smile monologue's rumination
sweetly mourning regretful Snapdragon.

PC

(Presto Change-o)

In the destructive element immerse that was the way.

—Joseph Conrad

Precaucion! Caliente prevarication's carton-pierre
charlatan polarized compass

pawning convivial pleasantry carbines
and pedantically Chaldee paraphrasing candor
a polyester choke pear chocked plebeian capacity's
plausibly conditional proof composite.

Proclaiming a corollarily postural charybdis
per the contrarily paternal Canaanite packs
Chia petting a Cerberus Pentium's
centrally processed carnivore perdition cuspid
and pinging the coltan personal computer port's
cabled pandora cube poisoning cochleas,
and phone charging the polity's
copacetically palatable cogitative parenthesis,
comma,

Patsy Cline's polysemically cognate, pachyderm-
congresses passing a cyclops philistine christened,
prejudice cursed pop cult's poser context prison cell.

Pure cement paste and copyrighted practically
a cheek puckering cog person's copious poop chute-
PVC clogging poppy-cock prose column.

Polite and credulous
presuming cordial populous convo's proper couth

publicly condoning Pontiac compensation's Parisian
cuisine Pedro-Carlos prep cooking pasta corporate
pension's ceramic piggy cornucopia.

The pill capita practicality's Celtic Pride circumference
pie chart probability cutting Peace's Corp, poor colored
people's champ pugilists crusading the pyrrhically claustrophobic protocol's contagious perception China.

Porcelain confined picket concepts paralyzing the conscious-proprietary and contravening pine cones.

Proprietor coms protecting the collusively presupposed capital
profiting commies pomp and circumstantial phenomena
counseling the pretentious Colin Powell coon piccaninnies-class prodding a contemporary pigeon crust pecking count's
potassium chloride Planter's cashew.

Paltry commerce promoting a crumb's positive contact
and pressure cooking a putz combustion.

The philanthropically crooked pilgrim categorical's
Pinocchio congesting pollen clime pledging a cross ponzi's
couch potato comfort parameter credo.

Privileged chauvinists pubescently comparing penile centimeters
philander Cupid's prurient chivalry procrustean.

Cinderella's partisan curfew proscribing cheekiness Ptolemy.

The Cheops Polyponesia's chemi-pyro catacombed proctor cliche-
and pediatric college prodigy concerns placating Caribbean
parables, cheering a Patriot's contest,
and programming the Chicago problem's cover.

A proxy condescending peculiar cantaloupes of Philando
Castille policed Canfields

perhaps a calmly placid,
cool and pacified coup–
pretending civility's plural courtesies.

The patently concise pupil curiosity's pace card poker chip
playfully called politically correct period.
Close punctuation.
Clap.

esp

The bearings of this observation lays in the application of it.

—Charles Dickens

Exia Shannon pantamorph of the Egypt Sakara
primed electric spire's effulgently subcutaneous
peptide and epiphany suction prowess.

Ephemera smart phone eruption service
providing "eurekas,"
sudden possession,
and the epigene signaled pulsars
of exponential salience
producing an extra strength.

Pineal electrodes streaming psychic entity synthesis
of a prismatically encrypted stellar particle
extending synapse prophecy.

Extemporaneous surpassing of the physically endowed/
solar-plex-emo synopsis, presently expanding
sagely palpable and exaggerating sagaciously
pre-emptive sibyl parallax effusion.

Spiraling purlieu ensconced shekinah pyre's
empathetically surrogate perihelion of e squared
projecting eleven.

Saphira's pearl extraction satellite par equinox,
solstice,
and plasma elevated savvy's plateauing euphoria
of a subtly polar expose.

Surge prominence of ein sof portal's emerald
samadhi prism elutriating summa photons,

and elucidating seen phenomena esoterics
seconds prior experienced situations peak evident.

Sheer pleroma evoking Siddartha's plumed exegesis
or summary precipitate.

Ether syncretized patterns of the endorphin-
savant polygon. Enveloped and siphoning prana's
elastic stratus phere emanations of silver parabola,
edifying Samsara's plane.

faQ

As soon as questions of will or decision or reason or chance of action arise, human science is at a loss.

—Noam Chomsky

Free association qasida's fait accompli
qualifying the fontanel anterior quickening
frequency amplified in quartz fasting.

Anahata's quasi falcon azimuth quotient,
fusion of alchemical quiet's fuming alphabet,
and qabala funneled anti-matter quote-
fleeing an aquarium-quercine flora's astral quorum
filtering ajna's quasi free assoc qasida's fait accompli.

Quite frankly awakened querent fractile afflatus
and a quintillionth fortified arabesque.
Quatrain of Fruitvale's archaeology quota flexing
an akashic Quashie's font arcanum quiver.

Flint arrow quip fortissimo of arithmetic quill fountains
and atramentous quasar.
Frescoed astrals quite frankly.

An asana's quasi free assoc qasida
and ferocious alkaline.

Quilted fantasm of aerosol qi.
The fugasi archon quitclaim.

ZZZ

To those who in the sleepy region stay, lulled by the singer of an empty day.

—William Morris

Zoiks Zora! -Zeruf ziplocked zanza zerstreut

zinging Zadkiel's zamboni zealot zouave Zimmermans

zenoing a zucchetto zizith zeitgeist-

and zonating zazen-zodiac zit-zoster zerlichs-

zig zagging zoloft Z-zoos.

Zolazoxamine zevving the Zurich Zelda zygote's-

zetetic Zsa Zsa zori zenith.

A zaffer zugzwang,

zambur zeppelin zornigs zapping Zulu Zale's zillah zloty

and a zillion-zechinned zinc zirconia zip a zany zakat-

zazzled Zarqawi zerosum

zaxing zen zubrick's zoetic zesto-causis zunehmend.

Zoiks Zora!- Zinnia ziplocked zymbelist zarzuela

and zinfandel zooted zaddikim zero-

zyklon zollvercin zephyr zorils

zestfully zooming Zapata zoetrope Zorros

zilch zonking the Zohar zombie Zeus zaddakkah!

psa

If ant colonies are viewed as organisms, a worker's death is of no more consequence than a man cutting his finger.

—Mark W. Moffit

Pete Seeger anthem's panegyrical sophomore ant parable,

scouring the Amazon paged sylvan artifi's pedogenesis stone.

Atheist progression soiling the ageist philos and

swarming an abridged pandect sanative's-Amerigo pie snippet,

ascending paper sprigged astigmia's prairie-

and secreting alpine putative's social agrology postern scenics.

The arduous provender steeped auspices in plastic streamer

of amour propre seism and abysmal pit slippage.

Almost plant stow away's pinch starved aner petri,

scouting aphid pastures and a scroll abridged Pete Seeger

anthem pruning sonar appetites.

Parading sextet appendages prance sapropel armies of pismire
suffusion, agnatic porters subsisting an agricult's plexi-suggestion,
always pupa stage

analogized pip squeaks, ambulating a peat soiled,
Archimedes principle of spit avoidance and Puma shoe

acrobatically, pachys slurp antibodies from pine sap
awaiting the pest solution anvil prostrating subterranean-
asphalt pharaohs shrunken accidentally.

Fdr

Periodically, a President will appoint someone whose background offends libertarians, as when Franklin D. Roosevelt found that former Ku Klux Klan membership was no impediment to Hugo L Black's appointment to the United States Supreme Court.

—Bruce Wright

Foot dragger rejoiced forty's don recipe
for disaster-rife Fed debenture and
Roman fleuve demogorgon rigging
of the family dime residual
fabulation darning Robert Forbes's dragon running
Fujian dust.

Rackets finagled doe repatriation
furthering a dysphemic retinue's Francis
Drake refrain.

Facon de rebus flogging dialectic remunerated
Fred Douglass's reproved fetter
and dextrose reaping fiat-
dominions to reinforce forbears,

Democrats retrenched filial darling reelection
flying a Dutchman's rat fink diadem rota.

From Dutchess region floated Dumbo Republica's
first demosthenes rogator, flossin' decade regality
for drudging a rough Florida district rally's
fuddy duddy renown, faithfully ducking a
revolvers five discharged rounds

Famously drenched rosary in the fire drake
raising Friar Dixon racist to federal docket robe
and foot dragger's rejoiced flunkies

and disingenuous resigned to fan dried Rosewood.
Fumbling doofus resuscitated a farthing's dip,
righting Freya's debacle, and

revived the fancy dressed raglan's
Franciscan diocese rectoring.

Faint draws to resile and fainteanize defect
of a Rotterdam feud dodger's reply-
fending the dawdle, and reluctant to forward
Downing Road's flotilla Destroyer rental-

fealty dredging the Royal Fleet's drowning rope-
friendship duet to revenge France's Dunkirk retreat.

And fearing a drubbing-
the recipe for disastrous response,
Fuchido dropped R-1 flotsam, despoiling regattas,
and the fatuously damnable renitence of foot dragger's
rejoiced finally, as the dapper roaring forties don-
riantly fought das Reich's Friedrich Dirksen,
Rhine federating Duce's rocket fascists.

Ribbentrop flew dogged, razing forfeited dock,
Repulser,
and fallow deer ramparts to flagellate Devonshire
ruin facilitating Danubian raids.

A foreshadowing of Detroit rubble's facon de rebus,
Ford donned reconnaissance-factory dispatching
Raytheon's festooned Daisy rifles-

and foundry dome rigamarole's flintlock disillusioned raff
fetching the dragoon resting Flag draped regalia
for Davidson's regiment.

Foiled detachments on Rayastan's front dexterous and rapacious,
a fad diet recipe for disastrous recruit fodder and
doubled rail fare dollar revenue.

"Rum filtrate declivity," roared forties don, Richmond's
fuhrer demonizing reefer and foot draggers rejoiced
foisted divesdom reserve's festering

The detente riff fling's discordant ricochet and fallacious
duties of regent flatly dashing the Rabbi Falasha's DC return
feigning to deport Rasheed-
for defending ranch on foreign domain.

A rippling fiscal diaphoria's roiling
and flumma diddle radio's FM dial reaches furnished the dialogue
rhetoric fuelling Dwight's riparian frenzied D-day retaliation
fullisading Dover's rivulet,
and ferrying DeGaulle's restoration.

Following Dresden's requiem,
fungible deferment reverberates founded dominoes and the
revamped FICA deduction retirement,
fixing deposits and a reimbursement future's
dependably rich food desert ruler's,
frankly despots,
the remorseless faitors de rigueur
and facon de rebus for Davidson's regiment.

USA

You're still in prison. That's what America means, prison.

—Malcolm X

The uxoricide of a statue Aphrodite's
umbrage, sailors and Aztecs.

"Uh-oh, Skipper," another ungothroughable-
stream aligning undulation of a Saragossa-
adventure's under shot ark
and upland societe anonyme's undoing of
the sixth Alexander's Unam Sanctum.

Awash and uncharted sod's ablocatio.

Umbilically, Saxony's Anglican Unitary
shored as usual suspects,

the Anabaps ullaged sustenance after an
ugging scarcity anchored-
and the ultrafidian settlers ate umpteen
sooner acolytes-like Upton Sinclair's angus,
umbraging a statue Aphrodite.

Uxoricide of a synoditie advanced the upstart,
supplanted Arawaks,
and undermined the Seneca Allegheny.

Upon straddling Appalachia urgently,
Sam Adams ushered the stamp actor's
utterly seditious abstemia.

Usquebaugh and suffrage's annexed utopia-
sank,
agglutinated Urdu,
and said Abe to Uncle Sawyer asientos'
ubiquitous servitude and acculturation
of the ulotrichous.

Sudra Africanos Ulsterman shipped across-
the ululation.

Sea Atlantis uncorked Savannah apparition,
and unleashed Sundiata's anthropomorphic
ubiety
through a sterile agenda's uterus splashing
amnio.

Umi says, allegedly Ulysses Simpson abolished
Ubangi Shari abduction
and unified the Sumpter apologist urchins'
supposed Appomatox urged superficies.

But alas,
ubi sunt acres unduly swindled in the accounting
of ulterior steed amerce usance.

Senates advocating usury,
stingy admins,
and ultracon strong arms of uranium.

Sputniks antithetical union shop aholics
and ultimatum sharia's alpha ursae superlative.

Accredited university shushed, allowing the Uzi-
student academy's uhuru sparse asylum and urban
sprawling auto

user smog absorbing the urine sewage aroma
until stock avalanches uniformly,

suburbia's apocalypse,

and the universe swallows approbation.
Uxoricide of a statue Aphrodite's umbrage-
saluting an advert.

The unleaded Shell awning uroboros, si,
an ugly sworn allegiate's understanding sabotage
and annihilation.

KKK

The third enforcement act, also known as the Ku Klux Klan Act passed on April 20, 1871 declared that Klan activity constituted rebellion against the government of the United States.

—Philip Dray

Kalon koniscope/

kerchiefed kazi's Katzenjamm kid-Klingon kerfuffling

Kibitzer koff kingdom-

kolytically kiboshing Kareem and Kobe's

Kwanzaa kairos

Kumbi's kundalini kennel

KAZAAM!!

Krest Kelvin karoo's kumbaya Katrina

keratomically knuckleballing a Kafkaesque keystone.

The koshare kampf kraut kaisers kiddingly kirtle kilting-

the kimono kicksie kempt,

Kleenex keepsake and knighted komodos-

Kelteching the kalpa,

and knouting kola kiosks a keelhauled kismet

The Kramer khatri kitishly knitting a killow Kwa klick-
kheda's kinetic keno.

Kayaking Kasanji klongs,
Kicheners kenspeckle a Kia knabstrupper, keeve kedging
the kalypto-kippa kirking, kepi ketcher kymorthas,
kvelling Kern's khaki Kickapoo king kraken and
karsting Keisha / Kevin Kline's kosher ketubah.

Kudos!!-
Kilroy kith-klavern katas, kneading kneeling Kikuyu,
knocking klaxon kraal's Kilimanjar kilter kowtow-
kindling Kentucky Kremlin's kerosine kindred-
Khoisan kaboom Krupp kits.
Katabolic keiselgur konas killing kaffir kindergarten
kite karma-
and kayoing karate Kwame's kofia a kittenish Kerrigan's
Karl Kani kloof   kookily-

The known Kali Krater's kleptomanical kyklos, Killian-

Kendal kniving kaleidoscopic Kodaks.

A kryptonite koine's krait kissing Kevorkian kulak kaliphate's

kickshaw Korean ketene kinda kindness

kurbashing Kweli's Khara-Koto K.O.S.

Kissinger's kitschy, kreatophygic kakistocracy kettling

Knoxville's kronerless kamikaze kleagle Koopa Kong komitets-

keeping kitana keloid kilns,

kidnapping Kuntas,

and knotting Kumasi's kinch kinte kernmantles, keenly

Kevlar kebobbing kenotic kinfolks kibbutzim kimbo.

Kneivel's Khorasan kiva kreiging Krazy Kat kermis kicking

Khufu's kinky, kemp keratin, kyrie koaning keisters kaput.

SOS

What before us lies the open grave?
Like men we'll face the murderous pack
Pressed to the wall, dying, but fighting back.

—Claude McKay

Solomon of Songhai and Sanjj onset's
sudorific SWAT opposer segueing-

Shinx olfactory security skeet and
Osiris's somersaltingly scripted,

owl skeleton shatter oath spree steaming

Olin shafts scattered the oval-
shelled ofay schism, skulls on spikes
and screwed the Oreida silencer
stealth occultly,
Sturm squoze oscar slack's
semiauto ochenta serial scraped
to Old Scratch sending
Opie supremacists sowing oats.

Seale six Oakland stockade and surplus
obliged saltpeter swap and the ominous-
safety switch open sesame spot-

on stadia scoping Squadristi skulls
on spikes, and spazzing out serene-
salvos offending the startled slim odd
sleepers.

Surprising opulent swine, stoic-
outlaw slayer severing olive switch

to sawed off shotty,
Shabazz ogling slatted shades,

Oh shit!

Senior O' Shea's sherlock obitter,
super soaking the orotund spilling
somatic ocean- spouts squirting organelles
and smearing seersucker outfits–

in summary snuffing obnoxious snatched Skittle
organ smugglers of Soter's ordo seclorum skulls
on spikes.

The slaughter of O.S.S.
obliterating a swastika's sardonic officers,
smithereening sarcophagi opportunely,
and swiveling Springfield or a Sig Sauer option's
street sweeper–
offering Shiva Shakti oblation
and swinging sweet oxcarts swoopingly.

Sniping Oz sorcerers,
Stono's ouster with shaven skulls on spikes
and splintered OTV shields.

Shaka oxidizing Spartan straggler's osteo-
sockets stippled to oblivion,
smashing oilcan swillers
and strafing the ornery stalwarts.

Staunch objection's ski stockinged operative,
staff sling onagers,
and a SR seventy one's Shakur sweetie omni spray.

Skulls on spikes and suffocated in odorous
sulfur of Sekhmet on Steroids, straight
outta STL's snubbed orifice shrapnel,

so Obdurman subversives shall overcome
splenetically obstinate Sumner-Steven
obstacles
and surmount shatan's oblivious snakes.

Sorry ovades Sayonara!

MiT

It is the age of machinery in every outward and inward sense of that word.

—Thomas Carlyle

Math inertia's Ted meet imploded Tesla-mistake ID theft
missiles-
irradiating a Tupelo mowed,
idiot throttle's mushroom-inebriation tangle-
metallically impelling trepannation's MK immersive
Titanic merger.
An indoctrinated twine matrix inveterate topical
motory's involunto-tendency-
merchandising intelligent travesty's
microwaved incapacity tepefied,

Machiavelli implanted theory minutia's invincibly-
Trojan marish Icabod transe minus if/
then meditations. Initially a tool of Menos's indoor toilet
Morse ignited telegraph mail improving a torpid-
man-industrial transit motioning international turbo
manufacture
and intensifying the twentieth millenia's incipient
T model imperatives to tinker

a monoplane's isagogic tiger moth invasion tune-
modulating instantly,
transmissions mutated into TV's Mennonite-
inchworming talkie marathon, inflecting text
message innovation.
Technically, a metaphrenic isolato's-
triangulated Marshall Island Tetris
manically inputting threshold minds
imitating thumb mackled italic type's MIDI inserted
telepathy.

The Mac “i” touch Midas insignia’s tabbied megahertz–
and an iffy tablet monger’s iron Tartaros maze.

Inferno trajectory’s monoxide inhalant tread-mill intran-
sigence of the tractable

molybdo infection and tactive memes tainting Michigan’s irrigated-tsunami-
milked-iodine-
toxicity.

Melted icebergs trickle a mercury ingredient tuna–
measure the Indian tromometer magnitude imbroglios.
Today
a military issue-tide-muck imprisoned tumor–
metastatically itemizing turgence.
Made in Taiwan.

WWW

You're not a man. You're a machine.

—George Bernard Shaw

Why Wilmot's wilting wrist watch wavicle won't wait whiffling,

whiffing weed whacked waxen Wisteria's woodbine Winston whippets

while the warva wiggle-Walmart work week's

Wednesday warehouse wage,

warping the Willawaw Woorali wattle weaving Windsor's-wanderjahr-Wangara

wagon welshers,

and wamble-woofing a wicked Wick-Wicky Whig witches whodunit wave-

length. A weltschmerz where wry warblers were wadsetting Wasichu.

Washington's whimpering Woodrow warrison wedging a widget-

wen wormwood weald, whose wunderkind Wolof watersheds wade the

wealreafer wallops and a Wasserman war whooping wacko's wankster-

wisdom whip-

whetstone whittling the Wonderlic a wan, Worf waffled whoopty-do-

whimpishly winnowing the Westinghouse wharf wreckage's-
wreath wizard webblie wave-

wrangling the wa'alaikum woosah's weathercock way

worsening-

whigmaleeries wittingly wreaked on the woozy, wonky,

and walleyed-warriors wavering wispy Walt Whitmanese whimsy

whichever Wakandan Williams won Wimbledon's Woodhenge. -Wishy-washy

whipperginnies and winsome wahini women wanna be wife wanigans without
    the want winces,

wrinkling a worry wart Willendorf weeping wah wah whistle waltzes-

watching the wobbly western's wild'n Winchester WASP wand winzes whirr-

wasting a wectare's wethers wondering what whelp will writhe a weak
    warrant's wager,

and whereby the Wilbur wisecrack warren woo's, a Wilmington-

wheedled Woolworth Wrestlemania, wedding Wakamba and the

    Weathermen's

Waterloo wrath Wellingtons and waking a world weary wordsmith's-

Weismannist-wiles, -wafting a Wurlitzer weighted-Wolfgang Weyer wiki

    welting a wealthy Walton whitlow's wallowing weasel-

wresting a wayward wino's-wifi-wavered wardrobe wampum. Wodey we're

withering wretchedly waxing wafer weanling waifs wrongly well wishing the Warner warlocks a whits worth,

whence Walden's wonted Welsing whispers wailed the whipstitch wastrel

wearing wingless Wu wallabees. Wink wink

BbL

There is a bar-restaurant in North Oakland known as the "Bosn's Locker." I used to call it my office because I would sit in there for twenty hours straight talking with the people who came in.

—Huey P. Newton

Ballot or buckshot lamenting by and bygone leopard-
Bobby and Bos'n Locker bar booth levitator's
barbed branch leaders of banana barge labeled bait
and bleached laity

beige bark lacerations
by and by Luxor's besieging became of lithoclast
buttressed Bantu logic briefs begetting Lavar Burton
brainiac loggerhead of balance beam leetmen boot
barack limosity.

By and by lazuli-boudler-beaded lanyards,
Basque beret lid and byssus barnous layering
the bonny babber-lipped baritone,
blatant luddite of baggy britch lint buying bodega lighters
and Bic burning the ligatures-borrowed barrio lien,

ballot or buckshot levying a bing bid lost boy budding
locusts and betrayal blooming lofty and buxom biting
liberals basically blurting Lyndon Baines bungled-
liberty-bell-bandaged-latrine brummagem
branding Lincoln the bald buzzard lattitude's
Bolshevik bully,

lionized by and by latewhile bogusly barked Langley's
bumptious babbit and larcenous barrator's beguiling legacy
of Ba-by-lon's bad blood liter bioassay
and the ban lieu bartered brick leantos.

By and by lonesome bullets breached Lorraine-
Belvedere's balcony of Luther by and bygone
libertarians burdening the Bircher lullaby-behooved,
be like buccaneer bullshit of Laney.

Bated breath lamented ballots or buckshot lugubrious,
but before long,
basement bolt lightning blitzed blank looseleaf
bridging a binary logarithm and becoming
the belesprit of Liquitex bravuras
blending largiloquent broadside bravado lipograms
and bold blessed leaflets blunder bussing
lethargic books barking loud then bitten by and large,
BWELL bypasses the literary bread butter limitation
befalling beatniks less bright by leaps and bound
buddies. Lo and Behold better lyrical Ben Banneker
layouts beleaguering the bush league basecoats
BEWARE locution buckshot

ballot lecture burying the barbarous lexicon burgeoning at
the bowdlerized library of bitumen blonde lore,
Bo Bo lynchings and Big Black Lies bozos believe
lucidly bringing Billikens lotus banned brahmin
leashes-
for bottling ballon libretto bard ballad lily bulb
bloom-litanies,
by and by lapel brushing backward Le-Bron basket
lemmas. *Bischi bischihk lepoeu!*

FYI

Already in speaking of shrines, of destiny, of the very Gods, we have visualized a succession of opaque containers rounded about hidden matrices.

—Judith Gleason

Fluidly you info for the yell in flatus–

yowled Indra's fricative yantra imanation

from Yahweh-imagined.

Fibrine yarned indigo fabric

of yesteryear's ibis fractured,

and yhlum integer fashioned

year indices flooded youthful ideation.

The fringes yanked inward-fesspoint

yawning inerrant and forgotten Yugas–

interjecting

foundational yardage is formed,

yellow iris flame,

and yearning flesh yoke of indelible falsities

yielding imprecation.

For your information.

GhB

There is a dreariness in dedicated spirits that makes the promised land seem older than the fish.

—Christopher Fry

Grifted her baby Gemini's has-been Guardian
hermetic borrowing Grandma Hattie's bleeding Grimaldi
hollow-boned gestalt.

Heirloom bastion from the Gael Highland being's
gamut heritage baptized a ghost
hybrid Barbadian Geechee and Ham

blurring a gauche hillbilly grafted half breed
gallerian of Hattiesburg grane.
A hijacked biped

grail harnesser of beached genome-hyphenation,
the balkanized Gold Hurricane begotten-
Grosbeak hitter batting gainsay handsomely,
bronze gethsemane hostage of blue green
horoscope battle

granting haters Blackwell of Ganges hermeneutic-beams
galvanized hydrolytically,
and broadening Granny's hasidic boat guided hotep birdie.
Grosbeak hitter batting grand Huebert's besetting,
gliding the Homerian breeze gusts, hell bent-
ghosting harvest borders
and glimpsing the Hapi basin's Guanche hermitage
gripping Hara's bow
and bidding grounded hoaxes begone
going home, bye!

All of a sudden they get together and start to move in a ring, round they go faster and faster. Then one by one they rise up and take wing and fly like a bird.

—Priscilla McCullough Darien

GOT

Glossary of Terms

A

absquatulate - *v., intr.* To depart hurriedly or secretly, decamp, abscond.

acrimonious - *adj.* Bitter in manner or temper.

adroit - *adj.* Dexterous; skillful.

afflatus - (Latin) **1.** Breathing, hissing **2.** The miraculous communication of supernatural knowledge; hence also, the imparting of an overmastering impulse, poetic or otherwise; inspiration.

agnomen - (Latin) Surname.

ajna - "Ajna is not the fontanelle or union of the coronal and sagittal sutures, which are said to be *Brahma-randhra,* but is the position called the third eye or *Jnana-caksu.*"

Alpha Ursae Majoris - One of the seven main stars within The Big Dipper or Plough. It is also one of the two brightest and is known as 'Dubhe.'

amour propre - (French) self love.

anahata - "Anahata is not the root of the nose, but is the spinal center in the region of the heart."

anthropoid - *adj.* **1.** resembling a human being in form.

aphasia - Partial or complete loss of the ability to use language, as a result of cerebral damage.

Archon - (Greek) The chief magistrate and after the time of Solon, one of the nine chief magistrates of the Athenian Republic.

arrogating - *v.* Undue assumption; the advancing of unwarrantable or pretentious claims.

Assiento - *Historical* A contract between Spain and a foreign country, or a group of foreign merchants, for supplying African slaves to the Spanish Colonies in America, especially such a contract in force with British merchants from 1713 to 1750.

atramentous - (Latin) Inky, ink-like, black as ink.

avoirdupois - **1.** Merchandise sold by weight.

axilla - (Latin) An armpit.

Azteca - A type of tropical ant with specialized plant habitations in the trunks of *Cecropia* trees. *Azteca* feed on secretions from the palmate leaves and raise sap-sucking insects.

B

babber lipped - (obs) *adj.* **babine** (French) Lips of a horse. Having thick projecting lips.

Babbitt - 1. George. The central character of Sinclair Lewis's novel *Babbitt* (1922), a self satisfied businessman who readily conforms to middle class standards of outward respectability and business success **2.** Any smug, self satisfied businessman.

barrator - One who deals fraudulently in his business or office.

belesprit - A clever genius, a brilliant wit.

bischi, bischihk - (Lenni Lenape or Pennsylvania Delaware) Yes, indeed (it is so)

bravura - Display of daring or defiance; brilliancy of execution, dash: attempt at brilliant performance.

Brummagem - **1.** A local vulgar form of the name of the town of Birmingham in England (Hence contemptuously) **a.** A counterfeit coin **b.** A spur.

burnous - A mantle or cloak with a hood. An upper garment extensively worn by Arabs and Moors.

bumptious - (adj) Offensively self conceited; self assertive.

byssus - An exceedingly fine and valuable textile fibre and fabric known to the ancients; apparently the word was used, or misused, of various substances, linen, cotton, and silk. But it denoted properly (as shown by recent microscopic examination of mummy-cloths) a kind of flax, and thence translated in the English bible 'fine linen.'

C

caftan - *n.* **2. a.** A long, loose dress. **b** a loose shirt or top.

canard - *n.* An unfounded rumor or story.

capricious - *adj.* **2.** irregular; unpredictable.

carcinogenic - *adj.* Having the potential to cause cancer.

cartography - *n.* The science or practice of map drawing.

centrifugal - *adj.* Moving or tending to move from a center.

charnel - *n.* A cemetery.

Charybdis - A dangerous whirlpool on the coast of Sicily (now Clafaro) opposite the Italian rock Seylla. Used allusively of anything likely to cause shipwreck of life, etc. and esp in combination with Seylla, of the danger of running into one evil or peril in seeking to avoid its opposite.

chassis - **3.** The base frame of a motor car 1903.

chouse - *v. colloq.* To dupe, cheat, trick; to defraud *of* or *out of*.

circumscribe - **2.** To mark out the limits of; to confine *(usually fig.)*; *esp.* To hem in, restrain, abridge.

claviform - *adj.* Club-shaped.

cloister - *n.* **2.** A place of religious seclusion; a monastery or nunnery.

coda - *n.* 1. *Music* The concluding passage of a piece or movement, usu. forming an addition to the basic structure.

compendium - *n.* 1. A summary or abstract of a larger work.

Comstock - Anthony Comstock was a dry goods clerk who lobbied a moral panic through the YMCA to congress. Comstock's nozzle refers to the Comstock Act signed by President Grant on March 3, 1873. It provided for one to ten years imprisonment at hard labor for transporting through the mail any obscene "book, pamphlet, picture, paper, print or other publication of an indecent character, or any article or thing designed or intended for the prevention of contraception or procuring of abortion. The original legislation authorized police assistance.

condign - *adj.* (of a punishment, etc.) Severe and well-deserved.

continence - *n.* **2.** The ability to exercise self-restraint, esp. sexually.

coquettish - *adj.* Flirtatious.

Crespi Effect, The - A disproportionate increase in habit strength as compared to increase in reinforcement.

D

Dachau - The Nazi concentration camp, with prevalent medical experimentation, where forty prisoners infected with sepsis were treated with biochemical agents. Other inmates were subjected to altitude experiments and injected with malaria despite no effective method to induce immunity.

dacoity - Robbery with violence committed by a gang.

Davenport, Charles - The Ph.D. biologist and mathematician, who was also an American member of the International Society of Racial Hygiene. Davenport established the Station for Experiment Evolution (SEE) and in 1910, privately funded the Eugenics Record Office (ERO) which joined SEE in 1920 under the aegis of the Carnegie Institution.

debridement - *Surg* The removal of foreign matter and excision of infected and lacerated tissue from a wound.

dedimus - *Law* [From the words of the writ, *dedimus potestatem,* Lat. 'we have given the power.'] A writ empowering one who is not a judge to do some act in place of a judge.
defalcate - *v. trans.* **2.** To curtail, reduce.
de rigueur - (French) Required by etiquette or current fashion. (sic)
derrick - **1.** A hangman; hanging; the gallows.
diaphysis - **1.** *Anat.* The shaft of a long bone, as distinct from the 'extremities.'
dolorous - **1.** Painful. **2.** Causing grief; distressful; doleful, dismal.
dolorously *adv.*
draught - *n.* **2.** A dose of liquid medicine; a potion.
dromedary - *n.* A one humped camel bred for riding and racing.
dulcify - *v. tr. literary* **2** sweeten.
dun - *adj.* Of a dull or dingy brown color; now *esp.* dull grayish brown like the hair of a mouse.
dyspepsia - *n.* Indigestion. **Dyspeptically** *adv.*

E

ebullient - *adj.* Exuberant; high-spirited. **ebulliency** *n.*
effulgent - *adj. Literary* radiant; shining brilliantly. **effulgently** *adv.*
Ein sof - *Kabbalah* "The infinite", "The endless", "The most hidden of all hidden."
elutriate - *v. trans.* To decant; to strain out; to purify by straining; in *chem.* To separate the lighter from the heavier particles of a pulverulent mixture by washing. Hence **elutriating** (sic.)
Elysium - *in Greek Mythology* the abode of the blessed after death.
empyrean - **A.** *adj* Of or pertaining to the sphere of fire or the highest heaven. Also *fig.* **1.** In ancient cosmology the sphere of the pure element of fire.
equipotential surface - A surface surrounding a body or group of bodies over which the strength of the gravitational field is constant.
exegesis - **1.** Explanation, exposition (of a sentence, word, etc.) ; *esp.* The interpretation of Scripture or a Scriptural passage.

F

facon de rebus - (French) A riddle.

G

gallerian - A galley slave.

gauche - (French) Wanting in tact or in ease and grace of manner, awkward, clumsy.

Gethsemane - 1. The garden outside Jerusalem mentioned in *Mark 14* as the scene of agony and arrest of Jesus. **2.** A place or occasion of great mental suffering.

grane - a snare trap ; a noose.

Guanche - \gwan-chay\ 1. One of the aboriginal inhabitants of the Canary Islands, who were absorbed by the Spanish on their conquest of the islands in the 1400s. **2.** Berber language spoken on the Canary Islands until the 1700s.

H

halcyon - *adj.* 1. Calm and peaceful.

hector - *v.* 1. intimidate by bullying; bully.

hermeneutic - (Greek) Pertaining to interpretation; esp. as distinguished from exegesis.

histrionic - *adj.* **2.** Dramatic or theatrical in manner. Related word: **histrionically** *adv.*

horrisonant - *adj.* Sounding horribly.

horology - The art or science of measuring time; the construction of horloges.

hortatory- *adj.* Of, pertaining to, or characterized by, exhortation or encouragement (1971). So **hortatorily** *adv.* (sic.)

hortum cultus - (Latin) horticulture.

haunch - 1. The part of the body, in men and quadrupeds, lying between the last ribs and the thigh : the lateral expansions of the pelvis.

haut - **A.** *adj.* High, lofty, haughty.

heuristic - *adj.* Serving to find out or discover. So **heuristically** *adv.* (sic.)

hyperborean - **A.** *adj.* Of, pertaining to or characterizing the extreme north of the earth, or (colloq. or *humorously*) of a particular country.

hypnagogic - *adj.* 1. Inducing sleep; hypnic **2.** *Psychology* happening while falling asleep; having to do with drowsiness or the coming of sleep, when the brain has difficulty separating reality from subconscious images.

I

in flatus - (Latin) breathing into.

isagoge - an introduction.

isagogic - **A.** *adj.* of or pertaining to an isagoge, introductory to any branch of study. **B.** *esp.* that part of study which is introductory to exegesis.

K

kalon - (Greek) The (morally) beautiful; the ideal good; the 'summum bonum.'

kalpa - In Hindu cosmology: A great age of the World: A day of Brahma: a thousand yugas.

karoo, karroo - 1789 (Hottentot of uncertain origin) The name given to barren tracts in South Africa, consisting of extensive elevated plateaus, with clayey soil, which during the dry season are entirely waterless and arid.

katabolism - breaking down process in metabolism.

kevel - a kind of hammer for rough-hewing or breaking stone. Hence **kvelling** (sic)

keck - *intr.* **1.** To make a sound as if about to vomit; to retch; to feel an inclination to vomit. Also figuratively expressing strong dislike or disgust.

kedge - To warp a ship, or move it from one position to another by winding in a hauser attached to a small anchor dropped at some distance; also *trans* to warp.

Hence **kedging** (sic)

keelhaul, keehaul - To punish a sailor by dragging him under the ship's keel with a rope.

kenosis - The self renunciation of the divine nature, at least in part, by Christ in the incarnation. **Kenotic** *adj.* Of or pertaining to kenosis; involving or accepting the doctrine of kenosis.

kenspeckle - Easily recognizable; conspicuous.

keratoid - (*Math*) Resembling a horn in shape.

kern - *Law,* vagrant.

khatri - A member of the second or military caste among the Hindus.

kheda, keddah - (Hindi) An enclosure used in Bengal, Assam, etc., for the capture of wild elephants: corresp. To the corral of Ceylon.

kibbutz - *n. plural* butz-im (Hebrew) An Israeli communal settlement, especially a farm cooperative.

kibitzer - *n. informal* **1.** A person who gives unwanted advise; a meddler.

kicksey (kicksies) - (slang) breeches; trousers.

kickshaw - **2.** Something dainty or elegant, but unsubstantial; a toy, trife, gewgaw. **3.** A fantastical frivolous person.

kieselguhr, kieselgur - A fine siliceous earth composed chiefly of diatomaceous remains, used in the manufacture of dynamite as an absorbent for nitroglycerin; diatomite.

killow - A name formerly given (orig. In Cumberland) to black lead, plumbago, or graphite.

kinch - A loop or twist on a rope or cord, esp the loop of a slip-knot; a noose.

kirtle - originally a man's a garment reaching to the knees or lower, sometimes forming the only body-garment, but more usually worn with a shirt beneath the cloak or mantle above.
kismet - (Turkish) fate; destiny.
kiva - a large underground chamber, often wholly or partially underground, in a Pueblo Indian village, used for religious ceremonies and for other purposes.
Klaxon - [name of manufacturing company] an electric motor horn.
knurly - *adj.* Having knurls or knots; gnarled **b.** Of the nature of a knurl, dwarfish.
Knout - King Canute.
koff - *rare* 1794. A clumsy two-masted sailing vessel used by the Dutch, Danes, etc.
ketubah - Jewish marriage contract or settlement.
kourbash, koorbash - A whip made of hide, esp that of the hippopotamus; an instrument of punishment in Turkey, Egypt, and Soudan.
kulak - (Russian) a peasant farmer.
kymortha - *Law,* A Welsh term for a waster, rhymer, minstrel, or other vagabond who makes asseblies and collections.

L

lachrymal - *adj.* 1 *Literary* of or for tears.
lacuna - *n.* 1 a hiatus, blank, or gap.
lalophobia - fear of speaking.
Lambert - The Lambert St. Louis International Airport. (sic)
lanate - *adj. Bot.* and *ent.* Having a wooly covering or surface. So **lanated** *adj.*
laniferous - *adj.* Wool-bearing.
largiloquent - *adj.* Full of words, that is liberal of his tongue.
la selva - (Spanish) the rainforest.
latifundia - Large estates. **latifundian** - Possessing large estates.
leet - (English) *History* **1.** A court held annually or semi-annually in certain manors: court-leet **2.** Its jurisdiction **3.** The day on which it met.
Leppoeu - (Lenni Lenape or Pennsylvania Delaware) he is wise.
lich - (Archaic) a dead body; corpse. A lich stone is a head stone (sic.)
limose - pertaining to, of the nature of mud, growing in mud.
lipogram - a writing from which all words containing a particular letter or letters are omitted.
littoral - *n.* **2.** The region lying along the shore.
logotype - A type of writing containing a word, or two or more letters, cast in one piece.

London & Sons - A restaurant staple in black STL specializing in fried chicken and ketchup served with french fries.
luff - some implement or contrivance for altering the course of a ship.
lugubrious - *adj.* Characterized by, expressing, or causing mourning ; doleful, mournful, sorrowful.
lunette - **5.** *Fortif.* A work larger than a redan, consisting of two faces and two flanks.
luxate - *v. trans.* To dislocate, put out of joint.

M

macellum - (Latin) (*pl* **-i**) a provision market.
macerate - *v.* 1 *tr. & intr.* Make or become soft by soaking.
majuscule - **A.** *adj. Printing.* Of a letter: capital.
manciple - 1 An officer or servant who buys provisions for a college, an inn of court, a monastery, etc.
mantelet, mantlet - (Old French) **1.** A kind of short, loose, sleeveless cape, cloak or mantle covering the shoulders.
manticulate - *Law* To pick pockets.
mantilla - (Spanish) Also **mantillo 1.** A large veil worn over a woman's head, and covering the shoulders.
marasmus - Wasting of the body.
martel - **1.** A hammer; after the 15th c. esp. one used in war. Martel as a hammer is an allusion to Charles "the Hammer" Martel who was a French military officer (sic.)
ma rupa sakti: ***ma*** - *Sanskrit* mother ***rupa*** - *Sanskrit* form ***sakti*** - *Sanskrit* power. Literally "mother form power" in Sanskrit.
marzipan - *n.* **1.** a paste of ground almonds, sugar, etc., made up into small cakes, etc., or used to coat large cakes.
maudlin - *adj.* Weakly or tearfully sentimental, esp. in a tearful and effusive stage of drunkenness.
Mauser - A repeating rifle having an interlocking bolt-head and box magazine.
maxilla - *n.* (*pl.* **maxillae** or **maxillas**) **1.** the jawbone, esp. the upper jaw in most vertebrates.
McCarthyism - *n.* the policy of hunting out suspected subversives or esp. Communists.
memento mori - (Latin) Reminder that you must die **2.** An object or emblem used as a reminder that all men are mortal.
mendacious - *adj.* lying; untruthful. **mendaciously** *adv.*
mens rea - (Latin; *Law*) the particular mental state provided for in the definition of an offense.

merino - *n.* (*pl.* **-nos**) 1. a variety of sheep with long fine wool.
metaphrenia - The mental condition of the individual in the modern state– one who is concerned with material products, is overly hygienic, is anxious, and whose libido is withdrawn from his family group.
miscible - *adj.* Capable of being mixed (*with* something).
Mohsine (Mohs) - Friedrich Mohsine was a German mineralogist (1733-1839). The Mohs scale is a metric for measuring relative mineral hardness.
molybdo - 1. (*Path*) Used in the names of certain diseases to indicate that they are caused by the presence of lead.
mordant - *adj.* 1. (of sarcasm, etc.) caustic; biting.
morganatic - *adj.* A marriage by which the wife and children, if any, are entitled to no share in the husband's possessions beyond the 'morning-gift.' Epithet of a kind of marriage between a man of exalted rank and a woman of a lower station in which it is provided that neither the wife nor her children shall share in the dignities or inherit the possessions of her husband.
moribund - *adj.* 1. at the point of death.
moskeneer - (Yiddish) (v) to pawn for more than it's worth.
moufflon - A wild sheep, esp *Ovis musimon,* native of the mountainous regions of southern Europe, as Sardinia, Corsica, and the Isles of Greece.
muladhara - Of the chakra system, the lowest center, where the goddess Bhujangi (or serpent) lies coiled round the Linga.
muletas - (Spanish) crutches (Spanish conversational guide). So **muleta** *sing. (sic.)*
muliebrity - *rare* Womanhood; the characteristics or qualities of a woman.
munificent - *adj.* (of a giver or a gift) splendidly generous; bountiful.
munificently *adv. (current)*
myotonia - abnormal rigidity of the muscles; muscle spasms.
myrmidon - right hand man, henchman, flunky, stooge, minion.

N

nadir - *n.* **2.** the lowest point in one's fortunes.
Nandi - The single mother of Shaka Zulu.
naptha - An inflammable volatile liquid (constituent of asphalt and bitumen) issuing from the Earth in certain localities ; now extended to most of the inflammable oils obtained by dry distillation of organic substances. Hence **napthene** *chem.* A liquid hydrocarbon contained in naptha.
natant - *adj.* Swimming, floating.
nautch - (*pl.* **-es**) 1. An East Indian exhibition of dancing, performed by professional dancing girls. **b.** A nautch-girl.

neap - *v. intr.* 1. Of tides : To become lower, to tend towards the neap. Also *pass.* Hence **neaping** (sic).

nefandous - *adj.* Not to be spoken of; unmentionable, abominable.

neologize - *v. intr.* 1. To invent or use new words or phrases. Hence **neologized** (sic.)

neoprene - *n.* A synthetic rubberlike polymer.

nephanalysis - rain map. Hence **nephanalyzing** (sic.)

nescience - Absence of knowledge, ignorance.

nidor - Now *rare* The smell of animal substances when burned, roasted, or boiled; a strong odor of any kind.

nimiety - excess, redundancy; an instance of this.

nisi - *Law* A limiting term added to such words as *decree, order,* or, *rule,* to indicate that these are not absolute or final, but are to be valid or take effect unless some cause is shown, or reason arises, to prevent this. Thus a "decree *nisi*" is one which will definitely conclude the defendant's rights unless, he shows cause to set it aside or successfully appeals.

nocuous - *adj.* Noxious, hurtful; venomous, poisonous. **Nocuously** *adv.*

Nodite - According Nuwapu cosmology, Nod was the biblical land of nudity. Hence, a Nodite is a nomad, of the Black Devils, in the land of Nod. Further, Cain was a nodite fugitive and wanderer who begat Enoch, which is a place name for Nod.

noesis - **a.** The sum total of the mental action of a rational animal. **b.** An intellectual view of the moral and physical world.

noisome - *adj.* 1. Harmful, injurious, noxious.

noology - The science of understanding. Hence **noologizing** (sic.)

norteño - A term used for mineworkers from the Mexican north. *Norteno* was not only a geographic expression, in contrast to the heart of Mexico, the north lacked a vigorous urban life, a strong sedentary Indian culture, and an economically vigorous church; its estates were mainly in secular hands. As a result, the conservative alliance between church and Indians common in the south was missing and, instead anticlericalism prevailed.

nostrum - A medicine, or medical application, prepared by the person recommending it; *esp.* a quack remedy, a patent medicine.

notandum - (*pl.* **-a**) An entry or jotting of something to be specially noted ; a memorandum note.

notarikon - acrostics.

novem - (Latin) nine.

nubilate - *v. trans.* To cloud; to obscure; to render less clear or transparent. Hence **nubilation** *n.* (sic).

nubile - *adj.* (of a woman) Marriageable or sexually attractive.
nuddle - *v. intr.* **1. a.** To push with the nose; to press close to the ground in this way; to grovel. **2.** *Trans.* To squeeze, press. Hence **nuddling.**
nugatious - *adj.* (Now *rare)* Trivial, trifling, of no comment.
nullipara - A female who has never given birth to a child. Hence **nulliparous** *adj.*

O

obturation - The action of stopping up: obstruction of an opening or channel (used in gunnery).
occlude - *v. trans.* To shut or stop up, obstruct (a passage), close (a vessel or opening). Hence **occluding.**
Old Scratch - (slang) the devil.
ophthalmic - *adj.* 1. Pertaining or relating to the eye, ocular; affecting the eye, as a disease. **3.** Affected with ophthalmia. *Ophthalmia also afflicted many Africans during the middle passage.* (sic)
orle - A heraldic insignia (Roget's "Insignia"). So **orles** *pl.*
orotund - *adj.* of the voice or utterance: full and clear, stronger than ordinary speech; also contemptuously magniloquent, inflated, pompous.

P

Pachycondyla (pachy) - A species of Nigerian ant, specializing in termites, marked by smaller raids than army ants. Pachys use individual scouts, which can reach 2 cm. long, to alert of possible prey and are known to survive driver ant raids with exceptionally tough exoskeletons and by playing dead.
Pandect - A compendium in fifty books in Roman Civil Law made by order of the emperor Justinian in the Sixth Century, systemizing opinions of eminent jurists, to which the emperor gave the force of law.
panegyric - *n.* A speech or piece of writing praising a person or thing; a tribute
parallax - The angular difference between an object's direction as seen from two points of observation, such as opposite sides of the Earth's orbit. It is thus a form of triangulation. Parallax can also be defined as the angular distance between two points as seen from a third point in space, such as the radius of the Earth's orbit as seen from a star.
patrician - 1. A person belonging to one of the original citizen families or *gents,* of which the ancient Roman *populus* consisted ; a Roman noble.
peccadillo - A small or venial fault or sin ; a trifling offense. So **peccadill.**
pedogenesis - Reproduction by animals in the larval state.

peregrinate - *v.intr.* Travel; journey, esp. Extensively or at leisure. **Peregrination** *n.*
peripatetic - **2.** *adj.* Walking about from place to place in connection with some occupation or calling, itinerant.
pismire - an ant.
pleroma - **1.** Fullness, plentitude; **a.** In Gnostic theology, the spiritual universe as the abode of God and of the totality of the Divine powers and emanations.
polyandry - *n.* Polygamy where a woman has more than one husband.
prana - Or prana-vayu is the subtle vital force in Indian theory.
prescient - *adj.* Having foreknowledge or foresight.
provender - **2.** Food provisions: esp dry food as corner hay, for horses etc; fodder, forage.
PTAH - The lord of life was one of the oldest and greatest gods of Memphis, and local tradition asserted that he was the creator of the universe ; his worship, in one form or another, goes back to the beginning of the Dynastic Period.
pulsar - A radio source from which receives a highly regular train of pulses. More than 600 pulsars have been cataloged since the first was discovered in 1967. Pulsars are rapidly spinning neutron stars, 20-30 km in diameter.
purlieu - *n.* **1.** A person's bounds or limits.
Pygmalion Effect - self fulfilling prophecy.

Q

qasida - *n.* (Arabic) A poem for a future patron.
Quashie - *n.* A negro personal name: Adopted as a general name for any negro.
querant - *n.* One who seeks to learn something.
quercine - *adj.* Of or pertaining to the oak; made of oak, oaken.
quorum - Originally certain justices of the peace, usually of eminent learning or ability, whose presence was necessary to constitute a bench; latterly the term was loosely applied to all justices.

R

recalcitrant - *adj. & n.* **1.** Obstinately obedient.
recidivist - *n.* A person who relapses into crime. **recidivism** *n.*
redolent - *adj.* **2.** Fragrant. **3.** having a strong smell. **Redolently** *adv.*
reticence - *n.* **2.** a disposition to silence. **3.** the act or an instance of holding back some fact. **reticently** *adv.*
rune - *n.* **1.** any of the letters of the earliest Germanic alphabet used by Scandinavians and Anglo-Saxons from about the third century.

S

saffron - *adj.* **3.** The orange yellow color of saffron.

samsara - *n. Ind. Philos.* The endless cycle of death and rebirth to which life in the material world is bound. **samsaric** *adj.*

sanctimonious - *adj.* Making a show of sanctity or piety.

Sanjj (Rebellion) - This was a rebellion of Africans enslaved in Chaldea (modern Iraq) in 868 A.D. (sic)

sakara - The kemetic concept that thoughts become things.

scruple - *n.* **1.** (in *sing.* or *pl*) Regard to the morality or propriety of an action. (current)

sephirot - From the hebrew meaning, "to count", "brilliancy", or "luminary", the sephirot are the ten emanations from which the ineffable created the universe.

Shangri-la - *n.* An imaginary paradise on earth.

Shekhinah - The "Divine Presence" exiled from Ein Soph when Adam was exiled from the garden. Shekhinah is an invisible flame. (sic.)

simulacrum - **2.** Something having merely the form or appearance of a certain thing, without possessing its substance or proper qualities.

Sirius - The star Alpha Canis Majoris, magnitude- 1.46. The brightest star in the sky. It is popularly known as the dog star because it lies in the constellation Canis Major, The Greater Dog.

Slay, Francis -Mayor of Saint Louis from 2001 to 2017 AD.

Sousa, John Philip -1854-1932; US bandmaster and composer.

spurious - *adj.* **1.** not genuine; not being what it purports to be (*a spurious excuse*).

squaw - *n.* Often *offens.* A Native American woman or wife.

stadia - An apparatus for measuring distance by optical means.

stasis - *n.* **1.** Inactivity; stagnation; a state of equilibrium. (current)

Sudra - (Anglo-Indian) A member of the lowest of the four great hindu castes.

supercilious - *adj.* Assuming an air of contemptuous indifference or superiority.

supra - *prefix* **1.** Above. **2.** Beyond; transcending (*supranational*).

surreptitious - *adj.* **1.** Covert; kept secret. **Surreptitiously** *adv.*

Sut-Typhon - Sut (Set) Also known as typhon, was a beneficent god in kemetic cosmology as late as the XIXth dynasty. However, when the cult of Osiris established Osiris as the "great god" of all Egypt it became fashion to regard Set as the origin of all evil. Originally Set, or Sut, represented darkness and night, and perhaps the desert, and was the opposite of Horus (light).

syllogism - *n.* A form of reasoning in which a conclusion is drawn from two given or assumed propositions (premises). **Syllogistic** *adj.*
synodite - (late Latin) Fellow traveler, traveling companion.

T

Tallmadge Law - On February 3, 1819, Congressman James Tallmadge of New York proposed that Missouri come into the Union as a slave state but that no more slaves be allowed to enter the territory. He also proposed that the slaves already there be set free whenever they reached the age of twenty five. The bill barely passed in the house, was defeated in the Senate and was raised again at the next session of congress, ultimately leading to the Missouri Compromise.
tabescent - *adj.* Wasting away.
taphophilia - A morbid attraction for graves and cemeteries. So **taphophilic** *adj.* (sic.)
telos, telic - pertaining to that which has an end or purpose.
tetanic - *adj.* Of, pertaining to, or of the nature of tetanus.
thraldom - *n.* Bondage.
thrall - *n.* One who is bound.
tope - A type of Buddhist tower shrine.
toponymic - **1.** The place names of a country or district as a place of study.
toponymic *adj.*
traduce - *v.* **2.** To pass on to off-spring, or to posterity, esp. by generation.
transmontane - *adj.* **1.** Dwelling or situated beyond, or on the other side of the mountains.
trepan, trapan - A person who entraps or decoys others into actions or positions which may be to his advantage and to their ruin or loss. *v. trans.* to operate on with a trepan; to saw through with a trepan, as a bone of the skull.
trochanter - *n.* **1.** A protuberance or process on the upper part of the thigh bone of many vertebrates **2.** The second section of the leg of an insect.
tula - In full tula metal : Niello made at Tula Russia.
Tulia - *Tulia Race, Cocaine, and Corruption in a Small Texas Town* by Nate Blakeslee is the story of judicial bias in the small west Texas town of Tulia, where in 1999 forty-seven people, most of them black, were charged with distribution of cocaine (Blakeslee). The convictions were subsequently overturned, therefore, Tulia is used as a metaphor for rural corruption in the criminal justice system. (sic.)

U

ugging - Dread, fear, horror, loathing.
ultrafidian - *adj.* Going beyond mere faith; blindly incredulous.
Urdu - **B.** *adj.* Of or pertaining to printed, written, or composed in, the Hindustani Language.
usquebaugh - 'life water' (Gaelic) Whiskey.

V

valetudinarian - (Latin) **A.** A person in weak health, esp. One who is constantly concerned with his own ailments; an invalid.
vallus - (Latin) a post stake.
vaticide - *n.* One who kills a prophet. **2.** *v. rare* The killing of a prophet. So **vaticidal.** (sic.)
venerable - *adj.* 1. Of persons : worthy of being venerated, revered, or highly respected and esteemed, on account of character or position.
venesection - (Medical) **1.** The operation of cutting or opening a vein; phlebotomy; the practice of this as a medical remedy. So **venesectionist.** (sic.)
ventral - *adj.* 1. Occurring or taking place in the region of the abdomen; abdominal.
verneuk - *v.* (South African Slang) to cheat, humbug, swindle. Hence **verneuking.**
vestigial - *adj.* Of the nature of a vestige; remaining or surviving in a degenerate, atrophied, or imperfect condition or form.
vicissitude - 1. The fact of change or mutation taking place in a particular thing or within a certain sphere; the uncertain changing or mutability *of* something.
virago - A shrewish bullying woman; a scold; a termagant.
visage - 1. The face, the front part of the head, of a person (rarely an animal).
viscount - deputy, peer, sheriff.
vitriol - 1. One of the various or artificial sulfates of metals used in the arts or medicinally, esp. Sulfate of iron. Hence **vitriol** *v. trans.* to injure (a person) by means of vitriol; to expose a thing to the effects of vitriol.
vis-a-vis - 1. **B.** *prep.* Over against, in comparison with, in relation to; also *lit.* facing, face to face with.
vivisect - *v.* 1. To dissect (of an animal) while living; to perform vivisection upon. So **vivisectioning.** (sic)
viz. - (or **videlicet**) *adv.* **A.** That is to say; namely; to wit : used to introduce an amplification, or more precise or explicit explanation, of a previous statement or word.

vole - One or other of various rat- or mouse-like quadrupeds, esp. The short-tailed field-mouse.

volitive - *adj.* 1. Of or pertaining to the will.

vulpine - Artful, clever, crafty, cunning, tricky.

vulva - *n.* 1. The external organ of generation in the female. Hence **vulval, vulvar** *adj.* Of or belonging to the vulva.

W

wadi - A gully.

wampum - Beads made from shells and strung together for use as money, decoration, or as aids to memory by North American Indians.

wangle - *v.* To influence (a person) to do something; obtain by scheming, etc.

wattle - *n. & v. intr.* Interlaced rods as a material for making fences, walls, etc.

wavicle - An entity having characteristics of waves or particles.

weald - **2.** A wooded district or open country.

Webley - A type of revolver made by Messrs. F. Webley and son.

welsh - *v. intr.* Fail to honor a debt or obligation incurred through a promise or agreement **2** fail to carry out a promise (to a person). **welsher** *n.*

weltanschauung - (German) (literally, *worldview*) One's total outlook or philosophy of life. Freud's later period is often called his *Weltanschauung* period.

weltschmerz - (German) Literally 'world sorrow.' Sentimental type of sorrow over the state of the world; sentimental pessimism.

wen - A benign tumor on the skin, esp. Of the scalp.

whangee - A type of cane.

whelp - 1. A young dog; a puppy **2.** *archaic* a cub.

whiffet - A small quantity of mist or cloud.

whipstitch - **2.** *as adv.* or *v. intr.* Expressing sudden movement or action. (slang or colloq)

whitlow - An inflammatory sore affecting fingernails.

widget - Any gadget or device

wizen - *v. intr.* Of plants: To dry up, shrivel, wither. Also *transf.* of persons, their features, etc. So **wizening.** (sic.)

Woodbine - A brand of cigarettes (*Wild Woodbine*).

Y

Yug, Yuga - (Hindi) *yug,* skr. *yuga* - york, an age of the world] In Hindu cosmology, any of the four ages in the duration of the world. The four ages comprising 4,320,000 years and constituting a *mahayuga.*

Z

zacaton - grass.

zaddakkah - *kabbalah* righteousness, charity.

Zadkiel - Pseudonym for James Morrison (1795 -1874), English astrologer used in the title *Zadkeil's Almanac* (formerly *The Herald of astrology*), containing predictions of the events of the coming year.

zamindar - (India) Formerly, a collector of revenue from land held by a number of cultivators: now a native who holds land for which he pays revenue directly to the British Government.

zareba *or* **zariba** - In the Soudan, an enclosure, usu. Of thorn-bushes, for defense against enemies or wild beasts : a fenced camp. Hence **zariba.** *v.*

zarf - (US slang 1960s) An ugly and undesirable man.

zarzuela - A short drama with incidental music, similar to an operetta or musical comedy.

zax - A type of ax for shaping roofing slates, having a pointed peen for making nail holes.

zazzle - (US slang 1900s) **1.** Sexual desire **2.** Exaggerated sexuality; sex appeal.

zeitgeist - *n.* (German) The trend of thought and feeling in a period of time.

zenana - [India] harem, seraglio.

zendic - *adj.* [Arab *zindiq* athiest] In the East a di-believer in revealed religion or a practicer of heretical magic.

zeno - Follower; cynic, stoic.

zeruf - *kabbalah* Esoteric alphabetical combinations.

zesto causis - To burn with steam.

zetetic - Seeker, hunter.

zeugma - *Gram.* and *Rhet.* A figure by which a single word is made to refer to two or more words in a sentence; esp. when applying in sense to only one of them in different states.

Zevlove X - Moniker of the Metal Face Doom as a member of the duo KMD.

zimzum - *kabbalah* Contraction, self limitation.

zingel - Perch.

zinnia - *n.* A composite plant of the genus *Zinnia,* with snowy rayed flowers of deep red and other colors.

zloty - *n.* (*pl.* same or **zlotys**) The chief monetary unit of Poland.

zoetic - Pertaining to life.

zoetrope - The "wheel of life," a mechanical toy consisting of a revolving cylinder in which the effect of motion is produced by pictures on the inner surface of successive positions of a moving object, viewed through its circumference.

Zohar - The Judaic "Book of Splendor," literally "radiance."

zollverein - A union of states for free trade among themselves and uniform customs rates against others.

zonate - To mark with zones. Hence **zonating.**

zoolagnia - Sexual desire for animals. So **zoolagnic** (sic.)

zori - (Japanese) A flat sandal, usually of wood or woven straw.

zoril - **1.** A skunk-like animal; **2.** A stinker, stinkard.

zornig - (German) *Music* Scattered.

Zouave - *n. formerly:* **1.** A member of any of certain light infantry regiments in the French Army, especially in North Africa, noted for their bravery and dash and distinguished by brilliant oriental uniforms and a peculiar type of drill. The Zouaves were originally recruited from the Kabyle and other Algerian tribes, later were chiefly French **2.** A soldier of any unit patterned on the same style of uniform, especially a member of certain volunteer regiments in the Union Army during the Civil War.

zoster - Belt, girdle.

zoxazolamine - A drug used to relax the muscles in treating certain forms of palsy, arthritis, and gout.

zubrick - (Australian 1900s) The penis.

zuchetto - *n.* (plural **zuchettos** or **zuchetti**) In the Roman Catholic Church, an ecclesiastical skullcap, black for a priest, violet for a bishop, red for a cardinal, and white for the pope.

zugzwang - a chess move.

zunehmend - (German) *music* Increasing.

zymbel - (German) *music* Cymbal.

zymotic - Contagious, infectious.

Works Cited

Allee, John Gage. *Webster's Encyclopedia of Dictionaries New American Edition.* Baltimore. Ottenheimer Publishers, Inc. 1979

Avalon, Arthur. *The Serpent Power: The Secrets of Tantric and Shaktic Yoga.* New York. Dover Publications, Inc. 1974

Barkley, Charles. and Reilly, Rick. *Sir Charles: The Wit and Wisdom of Charles Barkley.* New York. Warner Books. 1994

Barnhart, Clarence L. *The World Book Encyclopedia Dictionary Volume One A-K.* Chicago. Doubleday & Company, Inc. 1963

Barnhart, Clarence L. *The World Book Encyclopedia Dictionary Volume Two L-Z.* Chicago. Doubleday & Company, Inc. 1963

Black, Henry Campbell. *Black's Law Dictionary Third Edition.* St. Paul. West Publishing Company. 1933

Blakeslee, Nate. *Tulia Race, Cocaine, and Corruption in a Small Texas Town.* New York. Public Affairs, a member of the Perseus Books Group. 2005

Budge, E.A. Wallis. *The Dwellers on the Nile:The Life, History, Religion and Literature of the Ancient Egyptians.* New York. Dover Publications, Inc. 1977

Chaplin, J.P. *Dictionary of Psychology Second Revised Edition.* New York. A Laurel Book, Bantam Doubleday Dell Publishing. 1985

Dray, Philip. *At The Hands Of Persons Unknown: The Lynching of Black America.* New York. The Modern Library. 2003

Ehrlich, Eugene. *The Highly Selective Dictionary for the Extraordinarily Literate.* New York. Harper Collins. 1997

Ehrlich, Eugene. *The Highly Selective Thesaurus for the Extraordinarily Literate.* New York. Harper Collins. 1994

Eyedea and Abilities. "Music Music." *First Born.* Compact Disc. Rhymesayers Entertainment. 2001

Fagerstrom, Ron. *Mill Creek Valley A Soul of Saint Louis Second Edition.* Saint Louis. Ron Fagerstrom. 2000

Gaye, Marvin. "Flyin' High (In the Friendly Sky)." *What's Going On.* Compact Disc. Motown. 1971

Gordon, Linda. *The Great Arizona Orphan Abduction.* Cambridge. Harvard University Press. 2001

Gould, Stephen Jay. *Time's Arrow Time's Cycle: Myth and Metaphor in the Discovery of Geological Time.* Cambridge. Harvard University Press. 1996

Halliwell, James Orchard. *Dictionary of Archaic Words.* London. Bracken Books. 1989

Hamilton, Virginia and Leo and Diane Dillon. *The People Could Fly: American Black Folktales.* New York. Knopf. 1985

Heckewelder, John. *History, Manners, and Customs of the Indian Nations Who Once Inhabited Pennsylvania and The Neighbouring States.* Philadelphia. The Historical Society of Philadelphia. 1876

King, Stephen. *On Writing: A Memoir of the Craft.* New York. Charles Scribner's Sons. 2000

Kowit, Steve. *Complete, Pocket Crossword Dictionary.* Eighth Printing. Miami. Success Publications, Inc. Miami. 1976

Little, William and Onions, C.T. *The Oxford Universal Dictionary on Historical Principles.* Oxford. Oxford at the Clarendon Press. 1933

Mckay, Claude. "If We Must Die." *Constab Ballads*. 1912. Poetry Foundation. poetryfoundation.org/poems/44694/ifwemustdie

Moffett, Mark W. *Adventures Among Ants: A Global Safari with a cast of Trillions*. Berkeley. University of California Press. 2010.

Newton, Huey P. and J. Herman Blake. *Revolutionary Suicide*. New York. Penguin. 2009

Rabinowicz, Harry M. *The World of Hasidism*. Hartford. Hartmore House. 1970

Ridpath, Ian. *A Dictionary of Astronomy*. New York. Oxford. 1997

Rogers, J.A. *100 Amazing Facts About the Negro with Complete Proof*. St. Petersburg. Helga M. Rogers. 1995

Roget's International Thesaurus. Third Edition. New York. Thomas Y. Crowell Company, Inc. 1962

Spears, David. *Slang and Euphemism: A Dictionary of oaths, curses, insults, sexual slang and metaphor, racial slurs, drug talk, homosexual lingo, and related matters*. New York. Jonathan David Publishers, Inc. 1989

The Compact Edition of the Oxford English Dictionary Volume 1 A-O. New York. Oxford University Press. 1971

The Compact Edition of the Oxford English Dictionary Volume 2 P-Z. New York. Oxford University Press. 1971

The Oxford American Dictionary of Current English. New York. Oxford University Press. 1999

The Oxford Dictionary of Quotations. Third Edition. New York. Oxford University Press. 1980

Schaffer, Edy Garcia. *The New Comprehensive A-Z Crossword Dictionary.* New York. Avon Books. 1995

Seale, Bobby. *Seize the Time: The Story of the Black Panther Party and Huey P. Newton.* New York. Vintage Books. 1970

Simpson, D.P. *Cassell's Latin and English Dictionary.* New York. MacMillan Publishing Company. 1987

Starr, Paul. *The Creation of the Media: Political Origins of Modern Communication.* New York. Basic Books, a member of the Perseus Books Group. 2004

Washington, Harriet A. *Medical Apartheid: The Dark History of Medical Experimentation on Black Americans from Colonial Times to the Present.* New York. Anchor Books Random House. 2006

Welsing, Frances Cress. *The Isis Papers: The Keys to the Colors.* Chicago. Third World Press. 1991

Weyers, Wolfgang. *The Abuse of Man An Illustrated History of Dubious Medical Experimentation.* New York. Ardor Scribendi. 2003

Wright, Bruce. *Black Robes, White Justice: Why Our Legal System Doesn't Work For Blacks.* New York. Kensington. 2002

X, Malcolm and Breitman, George. *Malcolm X Speaks.* New York. Grove Press. 1965

www.ingramcontent.com/pod-product-compliance
Lightning Source LLC
Chambersburg PA
CBHW021950160426
43195CB00011B/1304
9781951960674